AYO'S **AWESOME** ADVENTURES
IN

BUENOS AIRES

CITY OF FAIR WINDS

WORLD BOOK

www.worldbook.com

World Book, Inc.
180 North LaSalle Street
Suite 900
Chicago, Illinois 60601
USA

For information about other World Book publications, visit our website at www.worldbook.com or call 1-800-WORLDBK (967-5325).

For information about sales to schools and libraries, call 1-800-975-3250 (United States), or 1-800-837-5365 (Canada).

Library of Congress Cataloging-in-Publication Data for this volume has been applied for.

Ayo's Awesome Adventures
ISBN: 978-0-7166-3636-6 (set, hc.)

Ayo's Awesome Adventures in Buenos Aires: City of Fair Winds
ISBN: 978-0-7166-3638-0 (hc.)

Also available as:
ISBN: 978-0-7166-3649-6 (e-book)

1st printing July 2018

Staff

Writer: Kim O'Connor

Contents

Introduction

Are you ready for an adventure? My name is Ayo. I'm an aardvark, a mammal that eats ants and termites. I'm also a tour guide traveling the world. I hope you will come with me. We are going to explore cities around the globe. Africa is my home continent. But in this book, we will travel to the continent of South America.

Today we will travel to the city of Buenos Aires. Buenos Aires is the capital of a country called Argentina. Most people here speak Spanish. That means most of the places we visit will have Spanish names. Do you know any Spanish? If not, don't worry. I will help you. I'll sound out words that may be new and strange to you. Let's try it! The name of the city is pronounced *BWAY nos EYE rays.* Neat, isn't it? Those are Spanish words that mean *fair winds.* When you tell your friends about your trip and use these new words, you will sound quite smart!

We'll also talk about many things that may be new to you. If I can explain these things easily, I will do so right where you are reading. If I use an unfamiliar word over and over again, I will put it in boldface (type that **looks like this).** All boldface words will be defined in a glossary at the end of the book.

I hope someday you travel with your family to Buenos Aires. You can ask to see the places we visit in this book! Then you can be the tour guide for your parents and brothers and sisters.

Buenos Aires information

- Population: 2,890,151
- Founded: 1580
- Economy: Buenos Aires is a port city. In the 1800's, trains brought farm products, especially cattle, to the city. Now the products arrive by truck, too. In Buenos Aires, they are turned into goods that people can use, then put on boats for shipment to the rest of the world.

Argentina information

- Climate: Mild, with higher temperatures in the north. Rainfall is lower in western and southern regions.
- Money: Argentine peso. One hundred centavos equal one peso.
- Flag: The sun represents Argentina's freedom from Spain.

flag of Argentina

SOUTH AMERICA

Argentina

BUENOS AIRES

Plaza de Mayo

History

Buenos Aires is almost 450 years old. That's a lot older than you and I, but it's still younger than many cities.

Before the city was built, native people lived here. Spanish settlers came for the first time in 1536. They fought with the native people, and the settlers were forced to leave.

Another group of Spanish people arrived in 1580. They settled near the place that is now Plaza de Mayo (read more about it on page 12).

The city grew very slowly. After about 100 years, only about 5,000 people lived here. There wasn't much to see back then—just a fort, a church, and some mud huts.

Those buildings are gone now. But we can explore a special museum that will take us back in time. It's called El Zanjón de Granados. That's pronounced *ehl zahn HOHN day grah NAH dohs*. I know it looks like a boring old house, but let's go inside. I want to show you its secrets.

El Zanjón de Granados

From the outside, El Zanjón de Granados looks like any other house built in the 1800's. But now that we're inside, we'll see things that are much older.

Over the years, many of the city's old buildings have been knocked down and built over. Only recently did people become more interested in protecting old places and historical things.

A businessman bought this house in 1985. It was filled with trash at the time. But beneath all that trash was secret

Tunnel Treasures

- Decorative tiles
- Smoking pipes
- English china

treasure—some of the oldest structures in the whole city. The businessman was surprised but happy. He wanted to fix up everything so that visitors like us can see what pieces of the old city looked like. Now, walking through this place is like traveling into the history of Buenos Aires.

The oldest parts of the building are the tunnels that we're walking through now. They were dug to channel water from the Río de la Plata. These arches and walls were built all the way back in 1730. It feels a little like a maze, doesn't it? I'm glad they added electric lights.

Casa Rosada

Plaza de Mayo

From El Zanjón de Granados, it's a short walk to Plaza de Mayo. It's the oldest part of Buenos Aires.

Plaza de Mayo is named for the protest that led to Argentina's independence. People gathered here in May of 1810 to protest Spanish rule. (*Mayo* is Spanish for *May.*) Since then, there have been many protests and celebrations here. Today this beautiful space looks much like it did when it was redesigned in 1884. Even down to the pigeons!

The huge pink building in front of us is Casa Rosada. Some people call it the Pink House or Government House. The original Spanish fort stood here before it was torn down

pigeons in
Plaza de Mayo

in the 1800's. Today, the president of Argentina works in an office in Casa Rosada. If we turn around, we'll see the Cabildo, the old town hall. It's the only building left over from when Argentina was a Spanish colony. Now it is a museum. And there on the corner of the plaza is a church called the Catedral Metropolitana. (You can read more about it on page 30.)

Soon after Argentina gained its independence, Buenos Aires began to grow. Plaza de Mayo was the center. The rest of the city built up around it. Let's walk to the Río de la Plata so I can explain what happened. But we can feed the pigeons first if you want.

Río de la Plata

This water in front of us is the Río de la Plata *(REE oh day lah PLAH tah)*. It looks muddy, doesn't it? Two large South American rivers, the Uruguay and Paraná, join northwest of here. The rivers' waters carry a lot of *silt* (tiny bits of rock) into this **estuary,** or natural bay. We can't see it from here, but the shores of the country of Uruguay are on the estuary's other side. It's too far to swim. Out to the east, the water flows into the Atlantic Ocean.

After Argentina became independent from Spain, its people could trade freely with the nations of Europe. The port on the Río de la Plata became very busy. People built railroads to bring farm products from

the countryside to the port. Ships took the products to the world. Argentina became a wealthy nation.

People poured into Buenos Aires from other countries, especially Spain and Italy. The population grew from about 100,000 in 1850 to about 1 million by 1900, only 50 years later. That was fast!

People who weren't dockworkers didn't spend much time by the water. That began to change in the 1990's. Lots of old warehouses around here were turned into restaurants, offices, and apartments.

The Illuminated Block

Our next stop is a quick walk from the Plaza de Mayo. It is the Manzana de las Luces *(LOO sehs).* In English, this place has two names: the Illuminated Block or the Block of Enlightenment. *Illuminate* means *to light up.* *Enlightenment* means the knowledge that comes from learning and thinking. Can you guess what happens here?

If you're thinking about school, you're on the right track. This has always been a place where people come to learn. Hundreds of years ago, the Illuminated Block was where you would find the city's first church, first medical college, and first bookstore. The archways and bricks remind me of El Zanjón. If we look for those details, we can tell which buildings are oldest.

By the way, there is a secret beneath our feet! Remember the tunnels we saw earlier? There are hidden passageways under this block, too. No one knows why they were built. Maybe they were supposed to connect the city's churches. Maybe they were built to hide things, or to help people escape from danger. We can't visit the tunnels now because they're too dangerous for people. But don't worry—I can dig you a tunnel later.

pigeon's-eye view

Avenida 9 de Julio

I'm going to share a joke while we walk to our next stop. Why did the aardvark cross the road? To get to the other side.

That's okay, you don't have to laugh. We're here! This street is Avenida 9 (Nueve) de Julio. That's pronounced *ah vay NEE dah NWAY vay day HOO lee oh.* Some people call it the widest street in the world. There are 16 lanes of traffic. So many cars are zooming by! Can you speak up a little so I can hear you? It's awfully loud.

The construction of this street started all the way back in the 1930's. It wasn't finished until 1980! The avenue was modeled on the Champs Élysées, a famous avenue in Paris, France.

We better wait for an adult to help us cross the street. We can stop in the middle while we wait for the traffic lights to change. Or we can catch a bus. To lighten traffic, four of the lanes were converted to bus-only lanes in 2014.

July 9th is Argentina's Independence Day. The name *9 de Julio* means *July 9th* in English.

The white, pointy monument in the middle of the avenue is called an *obelisk (OB uh lihsk)*. This obelisk was built to honor the 400th anniversary of the city's founding. Think of it as a huge birthday cake candle!

San Telmo

Buenos Aires has many different **barrios** (neighborhoods). The oldest barrio is San Telmo. We can get there by walking south, and then we'll turn toward the river.

For hundreds of years, almost everyone in the city lived here in San Telmo. But a deadly disease called yellow fever started to spread in the late 1800's. People wanted to get away from the crowded conditions, which helped to spread disease. Families who could afford it moved north. The houses they left behind were turned into apartment buildings. Many of the immigrants pouring into Buenos Aires found a place to live here.

I can tell that San Telmo is old because the streets are narrow and paved with round stones. In other barrios, the streets are wide, with modern pavement. Should we peek inside the antique shops? Maybe we'll take a dance lesson and learn the **tango** (see page 24).

I'm getting hungry, so maybe we should stop for a snack instead. It's a nice day to sit outside. Let's grab a table. We can sit under one of the umbrellas here at Plaza Dorrego. It's a public square like Plaza de Mayo. You can eat a *factura,* a yummy pastry.

factura

Plaza Dorrego

21

La Boca

If we walk through Parque Lezama, we'll be in a different **barrio** called La Boca. Many Italian immigrants settled in this neighborhood, so it is a good place to get pizza.

There are a lot of tourists here, so try to stay close to me. La Boca is famous for its brightly painted houses. Or at least that's what I've heard. Aardvarks are color blind, so I wouldn't know! Can you tell me which colors you see?

The most famous street in La Boca is called El Caminito (*ka mih NEE*

toh). That means *little street* in Spanish. The street is a museum in the open air. As we walk, we can look at the paintings and sculptures. (Don't forget to look up. Some of the sculptures are on the balconies of the colorful houses.) Before there was art here, people used this area as a dump, filling it with trash! Before that, it was covered in railroad tracks. And before *that,* there was just a small stream with a little bridge. I think I like the way it is now the best.

El Caminito became famous because of a **tango** song. The song is called "Caminito." It was composed by Juan de Dios Filiberto. The tango is a kind of music and dance invented by the **porteños.** Did you notice the couples twirling around while we walked down El Caminito? They were dancing the tango. The whole city is their ballroom.

Look, I see dancers up ahead. Do you see the man in the dark suit and the woman in high-heeled shoes? I can tell they're dancing the tango by the way they hold their arms and the sharp kicks they make. Their faces show so much emotion!

There's one last thing I want to show you in La Boca—a giant football stadium called Estadio Alberto J. Armando. (Football is known as *soccer* in the United States.) The team that plays here is called the Boca Juniors. The stadium's nickname, La Bombonera, means *chocolate box* in English. Some say the stadium looks like a giant chocolate box. But it's painted in the team colors, yellow and blue, not brown.

tango dancing

The club name says *Juniors,* but that doesn't mean kids play here. Argentinians love *fútbol* (soccer), and this men's team is one of the best.

24

Cultural center

Let's take the **subway** to zoom to our next stop. The CCK (Centro Cultural Kirchner) is the city's cultural center, a place where **porteños** come to enjoy the arts. The building is very big and grand. It takes up the entire block! Thousands of people come here every day for free classes, concerts, and exhibits.

The CCK opened in 2015, but the building it's in has been here for a long time. I can't remember what it was before, though. Let's hunt for clues to help jog my memory.

Look—I see mailboxes on the wall over there. And these long marble counters seem like good places to write a letter. I remember now! This used to be the city's central post office. When it opened back in 1928, it was the biggest building in all of Argentina.

La Ballena Azul

The CCK's main concert hall is called La Ballena Azul *(by AY nah ah ZOOL)*, which means *the blue whale.* It's like a big metal balloon on stilts. The design makes the sound inside just right. It's big enough to hold an audience of 1,750 people.

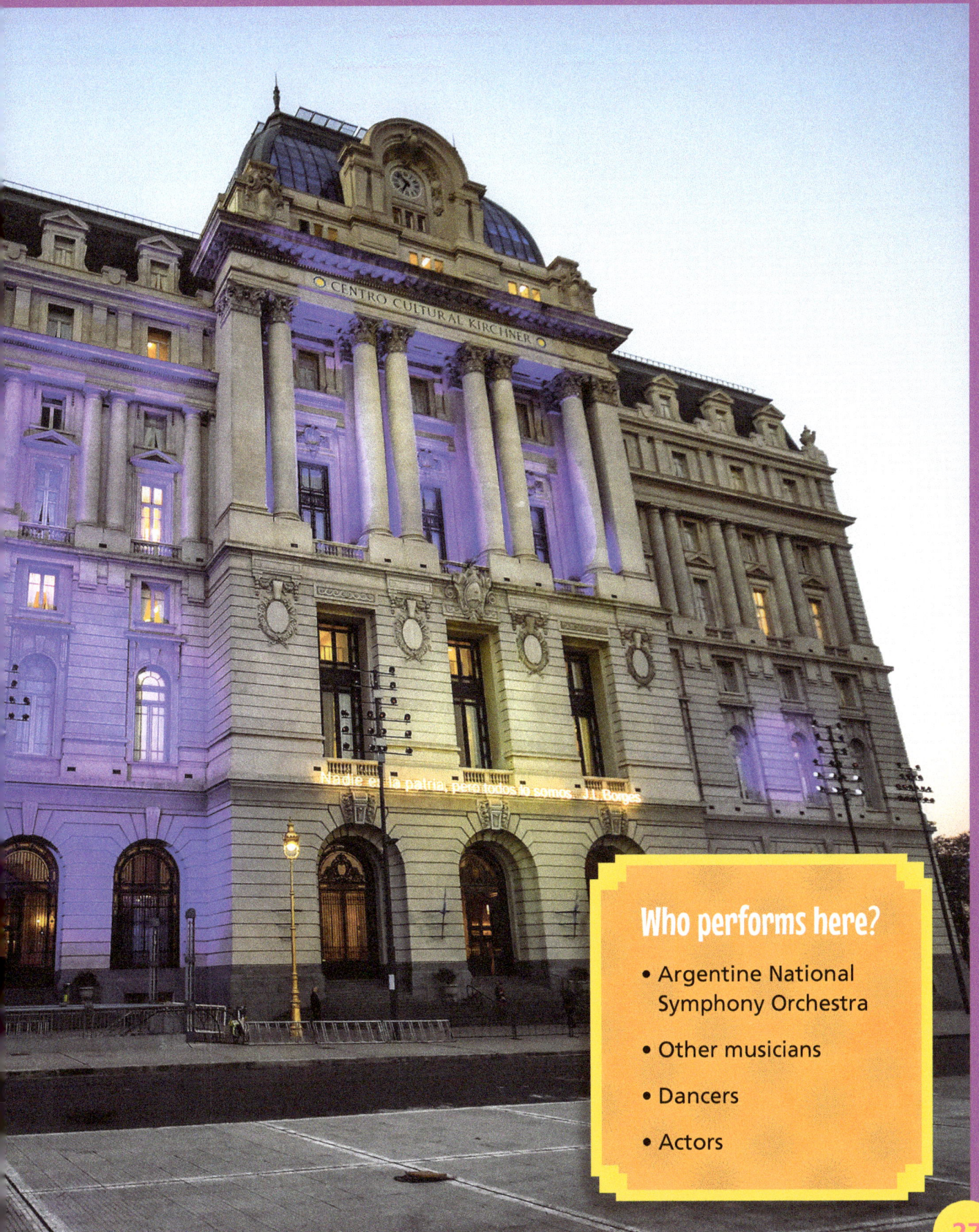

Who performs here?

- Argentine National Symphony Orchestra

- Other musicians

- Dancers

- Actors

Calle Florida

We've been inside for a while. Let's stretch our legs. This street is called Calle *(KY ay)* Florida, or Florida Street. It is a nice place to walk because the street is for **pedestrians** only—it is closed to traffic. There are lots of shops here, if you'd like to buy a gift for anyone back home.

Do you like to watch people? Calle Florida is a good place for that. I see a lot of people with shopping bags. (**Porteños** love to shop.) I see street performers who are singing or playing the guitar. I see workers in *kioskos,* little stands where they sell newspapers and candy. I see a lot of people in business suits who seem to be in a hurry. This is because there are a lot of banks and offices nearby.

Let's stop in this shopping mall. The ceilings are really something to see. This place is called Galerías Pacífico *(gah lah REE ahs pah SIH fih koh).* When the building opened in 1889, it was the Museum of Fine Arts. (The museum is in another **barrio** now.) There are still paintings here, though. Look up! Argentine artists painted 12 scenes on the *cupola* (domed ceiling). Have you ever seen such a fancy place to shop?

Galerías Pacífico

Calle Florida

Cathedrals

Most people in Argentina are of the Roman Catholic faith, so Buenos Aires has a lot of Catholic churches. The outsides of some of these churches look very plain, but others are quite fancy. We have enough time to look at two: the Catedral Metropolitana and the Basílica del Santísimo Sacramento.

The Catedral Metropolitana is the main Catholic church in Buenos Aires. The church we see today was built in the 1800's, but there's been a church at this place, on the Plaza de Mayo, since the first days of the city.

The body of Argentina's most famous hero is buried here. His name was General José de San Martín. In the early 1800's, he fought to help Argentina gain independence from Spain. Did you see the small burning torch on the wall outside the general's tomb? It is a symbol of the general's everlasting spirit.

To reach the Basílica del Santísimo Sacramento, we can walk straight north on San Martín street. See the three towers up ahead? That's it! (There are five towers, but we can see only three from here.) My favorite part is inside. The central altar looks like a white-and-gold wedding cake, and the floor is a *mosaic*—say *moh ZAY ihk*—pictures and designs made from many tiny colored tiles.

Catedral
Metropolitana

altar at Basílica
del Santísimo
Sacramento

El Cementerio de la Recoleta

Let's hop in a taxi so we can rest a little on our way to Recoleta Cemetery, in the Recoleta **barrio.** I know what you're thinking. A *cemetery* is a graveyard, which may seem a little scary. Please don't worry! It is a very beautiful place.

El Cementerio de la Recoleta *(seh mehn TAIR yo day lah ray koh LAY tah),* as it's called in Spanish, is like a small, quiet city. There's no grass, like you'd see in many graveyards. Instead we can stroll down sidewalks. These small buildings hold the bodies of the dead. We see many shapes and sizes. Some are decorated with statues of marble or stone. Each mausoleum seems to look different, doesn't it?

Who's buried here?

- Presidents
- War heroes
- Celebrities
- Scientists

This was the first public cemetery in Buenos Aires. It opened in 1822. Getting a spot here isn't easy! It costs a lot of money. But some of the graves are so old that they have been forgotten. That's why some of the mausoleums seem so nice and new, and others are dusty and crumbling.

I almost forgot to tell you about the graveyard cats. Do you see the orange kitty over there? He's napping in the sunshine. He lives here with dozens of his friends. Volunteers feed the graveyard cats twice a day.

Parque Tres de Febrero

There are a lot of cars in the city. Their exhaust can cause a kind of air pollution called *smog.* I think it's time for green grass and fresh air. Let's take a break in Parque Tres de Febrero *(PAHR kay TRAYS day feh BRAY roh)*—the biggest park in the city!

See the families having picnics? I forgot to pack food. But if you're hungry, we can grab a quick bite from one of the *street vendors.* These are people who cook and sell food from stalls or carts. Would you like to try *choripán?* It's like a hot dog, but spicier.

We can walk around the park while you eat. Up ahead is a big building that's round like a ball. That's the Planetario Galileo Galilei, a planetarium named after a famous Italian scientist of the 1600's. A planetarium is a place where you learn about the planets and the stars.

That sweet smell must be the Rosedal rose garden. We have to see it before we go. It's the most famous place in the park! There are thousands and thousands of roses—too many for us to count. I bet you can name the different colors, though. Do you see red, white, and pink roses? What other colors do you see?

What else will we see at the park?

- In-line skaters
- Ponds
- Pedal boats
- Birds
- Bikers

Planetario Galileo Galilei

Tres de Febrero means February 3rd in Spanish. On this day in 1852, a *dictator* (harsh ruler) was overthrown, and some of his land was turned into this park.

Avenida Corrientes

Avenida Corrientes *(kohr YEN tays)* is a long road that goes through the city. This is where **porteños** come to have fun at night.

Have you heard of Broadway in New York City? That's where you can see musicals and plays. Well, Avenida Corrientes is the Broadway of Buenos Aires.

There are a lot of people passing us on the sidewalk. It seems like everyone is dressed up! People are here to eat in restaurants, watch **tango** dancing, go to concerts, see a film, or watch a play. Avenida Corrientes is also known for its bookshops. Buenos Aires is famous for having many bookstores.

This fancy shopping center is called Mercado de Abasto *(mair KAH doh day ah BAHS toh)*. I want to show you this building because I like the curvy roof and the giant windows. It used to be a big vegetable market, where it was illegal to sell meat! These days, we can go to the children's museum or the movies, if we want to skip the shops.

Mercado de Abasto

Teatro Colón

The teatro's only flaw

The famous opera singer Luciano Pavarotti complained that the sound quality here was so good that people could hear every mistake!

This big building is one of the world's best opera houses. Opera is a kind of play in which people sing to music as well as speak, instead of speaking only. This opera house is called the Teatro Colón (pronounced *tay AHT roh coh LOHN).* Let's peek inside!

The Teatro Colón was built more than 100 years ago. It opened in 1908. I love the pink marble staircases in the lobby. You'll see lots of other special details as we walk through the building. There is stained glass and a *chandelier* (fancy light fixture) with 700 bulbs.

The main theater is huge! There are more than 2,000 soft red seats for the audience, plus room for people to stand in the galleries higher up. The theater was built so that it's easy to hear the performers from anywhere in it. The singers don't even use microphones!

A lot of things happen behind the scenes. Hundreds of people work in the building's big basement to make costumes, build sets, and do the performers' hair and makeup. It's like an underground city down there! I've heard there's even a shoe shop, though I'm not sure that they make aardvark sizes.

Pampas

I think it's almost time for dinner, don't you? On the way, I want to tell you about the *pampas* (pronounced *PAM puhs),* the wide grassy plains that lie just outside the city. If we had an extra day, I would take you there to see an *estancia* (eh STAHNS yuh). That's Spanish for *cattle ranch.* Instead let's use our imaginations.

It's easy to picture the land in my mind because it's very flat and very grassy. The pampas cover a big chunk of Argentina—nearly one-fifth! The soil here is fertile, good for farming and ranching.

Hundreds and hundreds of years ago, there were no cattle in Argentina.

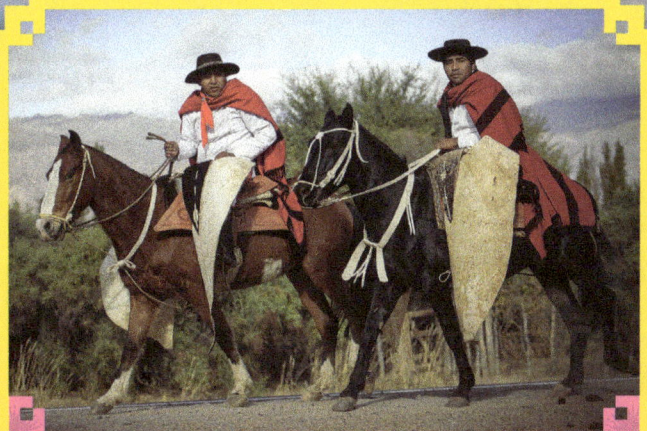

Gauchos once wore woolen *ponchos* (cloaks), baggy trousers, big hats, and bright scarfs.

The animals arrived with Spanish explorers in the 1500's. Can you guess what happened next? Cattle loved grazing on all this flat, grassy land. They roamed and spread across the pampas. Today, there are more cows than people in Argentina.

The pampas are home to cowboys called *gauchos (GOW chohs)*. Many gauchos have a mix of European and native ancestry. At first, gauchos caught wild cattle and sold them for leather, not meat. Over time, though, meat became more important than leather. Most gauchos started working for estancias instead of by themselves.

Dinner at the parilla

Let's go to a *parilla* (pronounced *pah REE yah)* for a delicious meal. A parilla is a steakhouse. The steak comes from cattle that roam the pampas. In Buenos Aires, there are many different parillas to choose from.

I know it seems late, but this is early for dinner in Buenos Aires. Most **porteños** won't start their evening meal until 9:00 or 10:00 p.m. I like their style, because aardvarks sleep during the day and stay awake all night long! I bet you're getting tired, though.

Let's take a look at the menu. I think you should get *carne* (beef). *Asado* is steak cooked over an open fire. You can dip each bite in *chimichurri,* a tasty sauce made with olive oil, garlic, and parsley.

If we stay here for dessert, you have to try *dulce de leche* (pronounced *DOOL say day LAY chay).* It's a sweet sauce that tastes like caramel. You could get it drizzled over a custard called *flan.* But I have a better idea. Let's go for gelato, a thick, smooth Italian-style ice cream. Gelato is easy to find in a city that has welcomed so many Italian immigrants.

Galerías Pacífico

Parque Tr
de Febrero

Avenida
9 de Julio

El Cementerio
de la Recoleta

San Telmo

Thanks for
exploring Buenos
Aires with me.
I hope to see you
soon!

Ayo

Glossary

barrio *(BAHR ree oh)* Neighborhood

estuary *(EHS choo ehr ee)* A coastal river valley flooded by an ocean. Most estuaries are shaped like funnels, with the wide end toward the sea.

pedestrian *(puh DEHS tree uhn)* A person who goes on foot; for or used by pedestrians.

porteño *(pohr TAYN yoh)* A person who lives in Buenos Aires

subway *(SUHB way)* An electric railway running beneath the streets of a city

tango *(TANG goh)* The tango is a ballroom dance for a couple in slow $^2/_4$ or $^4/_4$ time. The dancers mix long, slow steps with short, quick steps, sometimes making sudden turns and striking dramatic poses.

Acknowledgments

Cover © Eduardo Rivero, Shutterstock
Ayo artwork by Matthew Carrington

4-7	© Shutterstock
8-9	© Vladimir N/iStockphoto
10-11	Tanenhaus (licensed under CC BY-SA 2.0)
12-13	© Eduardo Rivero, Shutterstock; © Ed-Ni Photo/Shutterstock
14-15	© Franck Fife, AFP/Getty Images
16-17	Roberto Fiadone (licensed under CC BY-SA 3.0)
18-23	© Shutterstock
24-25	© Grafissimo/iStockphoto; © Holgs/iStockphoto
26-27	© SC Image/Shutterstock; Carlos Arias, Ministry of Federal Planning of Argentina
28-29	© Shutterstock; © Chad Ehlers, Alamy Images
30-33	© Shutterstock
34-35	© Bjanka Kadic, Alamy Images; © Nessa Gnatoush, Shutterstock
36-37	© Yadid Levy, Alamy Images; Nsimean (licensed under CC BY-SA 3.0)
38-39	© T photography/Shutterstock; © Angelo D'Amico, Shutterstock
40-41	© Yadid Levy, Alamy Images; © Shutterstock
42-43	© Shutterstock; © JM Travel/Shutterstock

Index

For further reading

Books

Caistor, Nick. *Buenos Aires: A Cultural Guide.* Interlink Books: Northampton, 2015.

Blashfield, Jean F. *Argentina: Enchantment of the World.* Scholastic: New York, 2015.

Brusca, Maria Cristina. *On the Pampas.* Owlet: New York, 1993.

Kalman, Bobbie. *Spotlight on Argentina.* Crabtree Pub Co: New York, 2013.

Websites

Guide to visiting Buenos Aires
https://www.lonelyplanet.com/argentina/buenos-aires

Information about visiting less-well-known places in Buenos Aires
http://www.atlasobscura.com/things-to-do/buenos-aires-argentina

Facts about Argentina
https://www.natgeokids.com/uk/discover/geography/countries/argentina-facts/